Dropshipping:

The Ultimate Guide to Building an Ecommerce Business and Earning Passive Income Online

Ecommerce Lifestyle Book 1

by

Caitlyn Rich

Legal Notice

If you enjoy discovering ways to make money with nothing more than a keyboard and an Internet connection, please leave a review on Amazon so I can keep these books coming. Nothing makes readers aware of good books more than an honest review. Reviews also help writers like me know what aspiring entrepreneurs want more of and how I can help solve those problems in the future.

If you are interested in learning more about me and how you can walk away from your soul-sucking day job and do what you love with your life, check out **Ecommerce Lifestyle**. There you'll find other titles as well as how to sign up for my mailing list so you'll be the first to know when new products are available.

The *Ecommerce Lifestyle* Series:
For individuals who desire to build wealth with an
Ecommerce Business and earn passive income online
today and always.

**Dropshipping: The Ultimate Guide to Building an
Ecommerce Business & Earning Passive Income Online**

**Blow Up Your Shopify Store & Turn it Into a
Money Making Machine**

**Dropshipping: How to Brand your Ecommerce Business
& Make More Money Than Ever Before**

Don't miss your free bonuses at the end of this book.

It is my hope they will assist you as you begin your journey to earning wealth online with your Shopify store.

Shopify Secrets *Cheat Sheet* & Shopify *Checklist*

Table of Contents

Introduction

You wouldn't be reading this book if you weren't looking for a way to earn money online. Maybe you heard some gurus on Youtube talking about how you can build a dropshipping business with little money invested. Or maybe you've heard of people who changed their lives by starting a Shopify store. Maybe you're just looking for a way to earn extra income to pay off debt or cash flow your way through school. You're not yet thinking about earning a million dollars in dropshipping. You just want a second income without a lot of money outlay.

Or maybe you are the one dreaming of quitting your job, breaking loose from the chains of debt and mediocrity and the nine to five life that stifles your every hope and dream, and living the life you always wanted.

Wherever you are in your journey, whatever reason you have for wanting to build an online ecommerce business, dropshipping can make it possible. It can enable to break whatever chains are holding you back. And best of all, those online gurus were at least halfway right. The threshold for starting a dropshipping business is very low, arguably the lowest possible. You can start your business without a lot of money to invest or a huge learning curve. Whether you are a beginning dropshipper or want to find a way to upscale your current online dropshipping business, this book will provide the information and inspiration you need to take your dropshipping business to the next level.

Why should you try dropshipping?

All you need to start a dropshipping business is a computer and an Internet connection. As long as you have a strong work ethic and aren't afraid of consistent work— because there is work involved no matter what some Internet gurus will tell you—if you're willing to give up hours in the clubs or running around with friends while you build your business, you can transform your life with a money making venture that can make all your dreams come true.

In fact, if you're willing to work hard and put in the time to learn the process of choosing a profitable niche and stocking your store with products your customers want to buy, you could earn a million dollars a year.

Yes, you read that right. A million dollars in the next 365 days. Even more. People are doing it with dropshipping every day. Every single day.

Why not you?

I'm not going to lie and tell you if you invest six hours a week for the next thirty days, within six months you can retire and buy your dream vacation home in the Caribbean.

A lot of gurus make it sound that easy. While it is true nearly anyone can earn money with dropshipping, it isn't likely to happen overnight. The occasional dropshipper has landed on a winner right out of the gate, but that's the exception, not the rule.

Like anything worth having, you are going to have to work hard to build a dropshipping business. Was that what you wanted to hear?

Are you tempted to stop reading this book?

I hope not. This book will encourage, inspire, and instruct you as I lay out what you need to know to get started. But I will never lie to you. Nor will I paint an unrealistic picture of how the business works or how you'll be swimming in money within a few months.

In order to succeed at the dropshipping business model you must be willing to forsake free time to build your business. You will need to learn a thing of two. You'll have to study and research and learn things you never thought about before. The whole process will probably take you out of your comfort zone.

You're building a business here. Whatever investment of time—and money—will be worth it when you are running your own online business and living life on your terms.

Chapter One

What is Dropshipping

Dropshipping is a method of getting goods from a supplier to a customer without them going through the usual distribution channels. As a dropshipper, you won't touch or handle the product you sell at any way unless you buy them yourself. You facilitate the sale. The customer comes to your online store, orders a product, and enters their mailing and payment information. The supplier fills the order. The product is sent directly to the customer. All the dropshipper contributes to the process is setting up an online store from which the customer can shop for the product they want.

Dropshipping is not a new concept. It has been around for a long time, and it will only continue to grow as online commerce grows. European countries are continuing to catch up the United States and China, the biggest online markets. According to data from the Office for National Statistics, online sales in the UK increased by 30% in 2017. That's only the tip of the iceberg.

Dropshipping is going to remain a hot ecommerce opportunity as more and more people globally move to the online shopping experience. Which makes it the perfect business for you to enter the online marketplace.

Major retailers have been dropshipping forever in order to sell products that are often too difficult, inconvenient, or expensive to stock in physical stores. Items that take up too much space or product handling to efficiently get it to the customer. Amazon sells items through this process. If you've ever bought anything from Ebay, chances are you probably dealt with a dropshipper and didn't realize it.

Many of us think of owners of online stores or Ebay stores as having garages and barns full of products waiting to be ordered. When an item is ordered, we imagine the store-owner handpicking the item from their massive and confusing stock and making a quick trip to the post office to ship it to the customer. This still happens in some situations, but many orders are fulfilled by dropshippers who don't handle the products.

This makes dropshipping a convenient and simple online business option for you, especially if you are just starting out in the ecommerce trade. You don't need a garage. You don't need a spare room to store items that may take forever to sell, if they sell at all. You don't need to sit in front of your computer and wait for orders, and then handpick the item and deal with payment processing and shipping.

The only thing you do is create a retail store, maintain it, make it attractive and user-friendly, and you will earn money. Quite possibly more money than you've earned in your life.

I apologize for this oversimplified definition of dropshipping. There is much more to building a profitable online dropshipping business than creating a store and waiting for the orders to pour in and the money to pour into your account. That's what this book is all about.

There are different means of creating online stores, but for the purpose of this book, I am only going to address Shopify stores. It's the most common method, and I believe the most user friendly for storeowners. We won't muddy the waters right now by giving you too many choices.

Just know going in, this business is not for the faint of heart. Or the lazy. Or those dreaming of making money by doing next to nothing.

Competition is fierce in the dropshipping world. There might be hundreds of other stores selling the same item as you. But as you will soon learn, those other stores are probably doing it wrong, giving you have a great chance of success.

Some of the items you stock in your store won't sell. You might not make your first sale for a month. Or three months. Sometimes an item will arrive to the customer broken or defective. Sometimes—even though you posted professional pictures and your product description was spot-on—a customer won't be satisfied and ask for a refund.

Despite all the obstacles, you can succeed at dropshipping. It is the simplest ecommerce business for beginners. It's also the simplest for those who don't have a lot of free time to learn a complicated process or deal with issues that can make running an online business too overwhelming or daunting to attempt.

You can do this.

If you are a college student working to cash flow your education, or you need extra money to pay off your student loans, dropshipping can make it happen.

If you have young children and want to run a successful and profitable business from home, dropshipping is for you.

If you need a second job, you can make a lot more money dropshipping with a lot less effort than you would working weekends at McDonald's.

If you want to pay off debt or kiss your day job goodbye, dropshipping is the simplest means of getting there.

You may be wondering, as I did in the beginning, that if dropshipping is so simple, why suppliers don't just do the dropshipping themselves. If you can find an item with a wholesale cost of $4 and list it on your Shopify store for $40, why in the world don't supplies do the same thing and eliminate the need for you?

The reason is it's much easier for suppliers to let you do the listing and marketing development. You create the beautiful website. You place the ads. You make the suppliers' products available to a global market. You get the sale. The supplier can focus on creating products and expanding their line of bestselling items.

Win/win.

We've established that anyone with a computer and an Internet connection can succeed in dropshipping. But you knew there was more to it than that. Nothing's that easy.

Let me tell you it nearly is.

Dropshipping has the lowest threshold for starting an online business. Imagine the upfront capital required to start a lawn care business. Or a restaurant. Or an accounting firm. Even if you operated the business out of your home, you would need equipment. Depending on your region, you would need to comply with building and zoning codes, not to mention health inspections, licensing, and additional staff for at least some of the work involved.

Besides a computer, which you probably

already own, you only need a few hundred dollars to get started with dropshipping. You could start with even less money if you had to. $50-$100 is enough to jump into the pool. To hit the ground running and upscale your store fast, though, you should plan to start with at least $300-$500. And after that, at least another $300-$500 per month as you pay for ads and business expenses.

It may sound like a lot, but it isn't if you compare it to starting any other type of business.

Many of us don't have a few hundred dollars laying around. That issue is easily fixed. I could write an entire chapter on all the ways— legal, of course—you can get your hands on a few hundred dollars by working a side hustle one weekend out of your life that will change your world forever.

I won't. Instead here are a few in case you find yourself with empty pockets but with the desire to start BIG and start NOW.

Forego the ballgame or barbeque or sleeping in and spend your next weekend washing and detailing cars in your neighborhood.

Shovel snow or cut grass. Walk and wash dogs. Babysit. Have a garage sale and clear out the clutter you said you want to get rid of anyway.

Do whatever it takes to earn a little extra money if you don't already have it. By really hoofing it and hustling you could easily earn $300 in one weekend. If by some chance you couldn't earn that much that fast, you could take a few weekends to do it while reading books like this one and stalking how-to dropshipping videos on YouTube. It's that easy.

The relatively small outlay of necessary capital shouldn't prevent you from starting your dropshipping business. If it does, you aren't that serious anyway.

The monetary investment isn't the only thing that can stop you from starting an ecommerce business. The time involved can also crush an aspiring entrepreneur's spirit.

Not one of us has a single moment more in a day than anyone else.

Fortunately for you, dropshipping doesn't need to involve a huge time investment. If you're willing to forego a few hours every night of TV time or setting the alarm an hour earlier, and maybe working through your lunch hour, dropshipping is something you can start and make money from your very first weekend. Once you start making money, a little money leads to more money. You can get your business off the ground and earning a steady income in a couple weeks, if not sooner.

It isn't outside the realm of possibility to earn enough money to replace your income within a few months. People do it every day. People younger than you. People less ambitious than you. People not as smart as you.

The threshold into dropshipping is low. The learning curve is low. If you want to use dropshipping to get your feet wet before diving into another ecommerce business, it's suitable for that too.

What Dropshipping is not

Dropshipping is not a ticket to printing money, though it does happen sometimes, and there are a lot of people offering courses who will tell you it is. Even those who seemed to make a fortune with their very first product, they put in the work and research first.

While a lot of people earn money their very first weekend—their very first day—don't expect it to happen to you. Especially if you don't have ecommerce experience.

You will work for your success. It could take a few weeks, a few months, or even longer.

Dropshipping is not for someone who thinks they can invest $500 this weekend and be making ten thousand dollars in a month. Or $10K per week three months from now. Or $10K per day three months after that.

If you're that person, you're going to be sorely disappointed. If you have such lofty dreams and aspirations, you will more than likely give up when things don't work out that way. If you don't make a thousand dollars by the end of this weekend, or $10K by the end of the month because you heard of someone on Youtube who did it, you'll get disillusioned and mad at me and quit.

Please don't misunderstand.

There is still a lot of money to be made with dropshipping. You can easily get in on the action once you understand a few things. But the people who excel are the ones who've already accepted it's going to take work, and it probably won't happen overnight or this weekend.

Lightning does strike, but you're not going to sit around and wait for it. You'll make your own electricity with hard work, smart decisions, research, and a willingness to learn.

Even if you land on a profitable product right out of the gate that takes off like a rocket, you cannot think that product will continue to sell until you're wealthy enough to retire and never need to earn another dime the rest of your life.

Learn this rule now: Winners don't last forever.

Business models change. Facebook changes their ad terms on a regular basis. Trends and technology and tastes constantly change and evolve. What's big and hot and a moneymaker today may be in the garbage heap tomorrow.

If you are a slave to trends and always chasing the next shiny object, you won't be satisfied with dropshipping. It won't fulfill your dreams quickly enough. Unless you are a celebrity or athlete that sets trends, chances are you'll always be just far enough behind to miss the opportunity to make money from it.

By the time most of us recognize a trend, it's too late to jump on board.

Dropshipping isn't for someone who wants to earn a fortune immediately and then get out so they can chase the next big wave.

If you don't make up your mind to do whatever is necessary to succeed, you probably won't.

Who dropshipping is for

Dropshipping is for people who have a business mindset who don't plan to hit it and quit it. Successful dropshippers plan to be in the game for the long haul.

How do we develop a winning mindset? By refusing to listen to the voices of doubt, usually in our own heads.

Voices that say:

You're not smart enough to figure this out...

You're not savvy enough to run your own business...

You didn't go to college, and neither did anyone in your family...

You don't have a business background...

You've quit everything you ever started. What makes you think you'll stick with this...

A winning mindset is essential for those who wish to succeed in dropshipping.

To cultivate a winning mindset, surround yourself with winners. I'm sure you've heard you are what you eat. You are also what you hear and the people you spend time with.

Positivity breeds positivity.

Negativity kills dreams and stifles your potential.

You're probably like most of us, and you have people in your life you can't share good news with. Some people only seem happy if they are draining the joy out of every situation. In order to develop a winning mindset, limit time with these people. Share your goals with winners. Chances are they have goals, too, and they'll be happy to cheer you on.

You might not have anyone in your life who isn't a dream smasher. Accept it and move on. Read inspiring books. Listen to podcasts from people who are successful at dropshipping, and keep moving forward.

Cultivating a winning mindset is done when we strive to provide a service to customers instead of just selling them a trinket that will go out of style next week. A seller who provides a service to their customers will be more successful than someone who wants to sell a product and move on to the next easy mark.

Winning sellers have the mindset of adding value to their customers. Whether electronics or gadgets that make life easier, or clothing or products that make us more comfortable and content, or something that provides the customer with more time to spend with family or on things that give them pleasure, they're all products that enrich lives.

Sellers who realize this and strive to provide value to their customers will be more successful and enjoy their business much more.

A smart entrepreneur changes and evolves with the industry. Like all businesses, dropshipping revenue ebbs and flows. You may earn a good residual income on an item in your store, but even bestsellers have peaks and valleys. You'll need to stock other items in your store that also earn a reliable income. When one product drops into a valley or is susceptible to the off season and another isn't as popular as it was last year, and still another becomes obsolete as technology evolves, your dropshipping business won't fall apart because you were prepared.

Thousands of Shopify stores open every day. Within 30 days two thirds of them are abandoned, many before they stocked the first item. Why?

Millions of hopeful dropshippers read books like this one and jump into creating their Shopify store. They love the idea of freedom and independence in running their own online business. They figure if their fifteen-year-old neighbor can start a Shopify store and make tons of money, it can't be that hard. They're smart, hard-working, tech savvy, and determined, so they jump on board.

They don't put much thought or research into planning what kind of store to create or the products they'll sell. They tell themselves they'll figure it out as they go along. They'll watch a few YouTube videos and fill in the blanks as needed.

It isn't long before they realize there's a lot more to the process than they thought. Research takes a lot longer than they want to put into it.

They stocked a great product, but no one visited their store. They kept the store open for a whole month and didn't make the first sale. Where are the customers? Their Facebook ad was great. They had an Instagram shout-out that should've propelled them to the bestseller ranks.

Instead, crickets.

Those who succeed at dropshipping are the ones who determine going in they are not going to stop and walk away when things get tough or if they don't achieve success as quickly as expected.

Success is the progressive realization of a worthwhile goal. ----Earl Nightingale

Success is a progression. Just because you don't get there by some self-imposed deadline or because things don't go as planned, does not mean you aren't achieving success. You are successful when you are continually progressing toward that worthwhile goal.

Be in for the long haul. Don't give up. Remember why you got into dropshipping in the first place. Was it to pay off student loans or cash flow college and avoid insane student loan debt? Was it to stay at home with your kids so you wouldn't miss those wonderful moments that will never happen again?

Remember your WHY. Keep it in front of you. Create a vision board. Record your goals, and make a detailed plan that keeps your moving forward in your business.

If you are willing to roll up your sleeves and work, learn a lot and apply what you learn,you can earn a very good living drop-shipping.

It can easily replace your job, unless you already pull down a million dollars a year. If you're looking to replace that kind of income, you can still get there. It might just take a year or so.

But if after some hard work setting up your business, a cool half a mil and beyond sounds good to you, keep reading. You may have found it.

Chapter Two

Choosing a Niche

The first thing you need to do, even before you sign up for a Shopify account, is to decide what kind of store you want to create.

You would not buy a hunk of land off the Interstate, break ground, and hire contractors until you knew what you were building. No one has ever driven past a construction site and seen a huge sign out front that read:

Future Site of ???

Builders know they're building a home improvement store before they design the blueprints. A jewelry store is going to have a different physical footprint than a grocery store, which will have a different footprint than a coffee shop.

Put some thought into the type of store

you want before diving into dropshipping.

If not, your store will fail, just like the architect who designs a restaurant and then realizes he meant to design a furniture store instead.

Before you decide to create a jewelry Shopify store because you love jewelry and think you'll be a master at selling it, there are a few other factors to consider.

Is jewelry a good niche to get into? Is everyone and her sister selling it already? Would anyone find your store in the overcrowded Shopify marketplace?

Think again of brick and mortar stores. A smart businessperson doesn't build a home improvement store sandwiched between a Home Depot and a Lowe's. They research first, and so must you.

Finding a niche that isn't oversaturated but still sells well will take up the lion's share of your research time. You may even wonder— the way I did when I first started researching possible dropshipping niches—if you're too late to the game. You may lament that all the good niches are taken. There isn't a niche or product left under the sun that isn't being sold the crap out of while you were sitting on the fence, trying to decide if ecommerce was right for you.

Rest assured, you're not too late.

Many niches *are* too oversaturated for a newbie. That doesn't mean your chance at succeeding in the health and fitness niche is next to impossible. It can happen. Just not today. When starting out you want to lower the bar as much as possible. That means carefully choosing a niche that will make it easier to rise to the top, not harder.

Don't go into the process with a product in mind that no stick of dynamite can blast out if the product isn't a winner. Your research may prove the niche you have in mind is best suited for sellers with more experience. Or not enough customers are shopping for what you want to sell.

You may have always wanted to sell cow statues for people to put in their front yards. You know there is a huge markup on cow statues. Each cow statue retails for $5K. If you only sell two or three a week, you'll be sitting on a goldmine. No one else is selling them. You'll create a market, corner it, and get rich.

Brilliant idea, right?

There's only one problem with your plan. No one is getting rich selling cow statues because no customer wants a cow statue in their front yard. Those who latch onto a niche they love—regardless of whether or not the market is saturated or no one is interested in cow statues—won't make money.

The next two factors are imperative when researching a niche in which to build your store.

The niche supports good converting products customers want to buy.

It's a niche you enjoy and have some experience in so you can easily sell the products.

If you take a tool out of an auto mechanic's toolbox and have no idea what it is or what it does, you're going to have a hard time convincing customers how badly they need it.

Yes, you can research and learn to answer every possible question about your product, but when you're starting out in dropshipping, you want to lower the learning curve as much as possible. After you've succeeded at selling a few products you know and understand, your opportunities will widen. As your sales experience grows, you'll be able to sell anything to anybody. Starting out, though, make it easy on yourself. Don't start with a product you don't understand or can't explain if someone asks. Because someone will ask.

You'll give yourself a leg up on the competition if you already know a little about what you're selling.

Occasionally someone lucks into a bestselling niche that sells like crazy. They fall into a product that takes off and makes them a ton of money with seemingly no work on their part.

Look at what happened with fidget spinners. No one knew a silly toy that cost pennies to produce would take off the way it did. I doubt most sellers began selling them on purpose. They happened to be in the right place at the right time and rode the fidget spinner wave to easy money.

Don't plan on an easy ride happening for you. More than likely, you'll have to research your butt off to find a niche that gives you the ability to stand out among the competition and still sell well.

Don't sweat it. This work is fun work.

There are online tools that help take the guesswork out of choosing a profitable niche. Since I'm not currently an affiliate for any of these programs I won't mention them here. Do a Google search to find spying tools before you begin your14-day free Shopify trial, if you choose to use one.

The clock starts ticking on your 14-day free trial the instant you sign in to Shopify with a username and password. Do some planning and research before then. You don't want to waste any of your free trial doing research.

You don't really need the spy tools, though you can check them out and decide for yourself. I'll do anything to save a buck, so I research on my own without added software.

The best way to begin anything is with the basics. Take a notebook or open a document and start brainstorming. Make a list of all the things you bought or used in the last week. Don't include toilet paper or toothpaste. No one goes to a Shopify store for those items.

Other than basic needs items, record everything else. Look around you. On my desk right now is a blue tooth printer, a bottle of nail polish, a digital picture frame, a small fan that plugs into a USB port, a pair of scissors, a pack of fine line drawing pens I use in my daily planner, and my phone. Except for the phone, any of these items would make great products to build a Shopify store around.

Make your list now. I'll wait. Don't stop until you come up with at least twenty items.

Now jot down twenty products you've bought in the last two weeks. Electronics. Gaming. Health care. Gadgets in your kitchen or on your desk. Home décor you can't live without or items that bring you pleasure and enrich your life.

Are you outside on your patio? Do you enjoy gardening or the peaceful oasis you created in your back yard? Do you own a pet or do you like listening to the ducks on your neighbor's pond. Do you hear wind chimes? Do you smell meat on a grill? Do you want to? How do you season your vegetables on the grill? What gadget will you use to test the meat's doneness? Do you need something new to turn the vegetables?

Now list twenty things you've used or spent money on in the last thirty days. For this third list, record items you've bought or given to other people. Things for yourself, your kids, your spouse, your parents, a friend's birthday. Don't leave an item out because you think you won't be able to sell it on an online store.

You aren't going to sell all of these items. We certainly won't be selling them in the same store. That would be a mistake we'll discuss later.

Now that you've made three lists with at least twenty items each, go over them and see which of those items you have the most interest in or knowledge of. This is important because it's always easier to talk someone into trying something you care about or know a lot about.

The point of this exercise is to find a niche that isn't oversaturated. The best way to do this is to narrow your niche beyond the most obvious products. Think of something you use every day and then niche down to a product that makes doing that task easier or better.

For example, let's go back out to the back yard. Your backyard or patio probably has a grill, some lawn furniture, maybe some whirligigs that move in the breeze, flowerpots, and a few gardening implements.

Impulse items make perfect products to sell in your dropshipping store. Like I mentioned earlier with the toilet paper and toothpaste, the most profitable dropshipping products can't be picked up at Target on your way home from work.

Stock fun and unique items in your store customers can't resist.

If you are stocking an outdoor Shopify store, think of unique items that would improve your own backyard experience? What would make it prettier, handier, more pleasant, or more comfortable?

Pretty cushions for your chaise lounge? A fanciful flowerpot? A cute dragonfly flowerpot sitter? A manly oven mitt or apron for the backyard chef?

There's a reason it benefits you to be familiar with your first niche before you start selling.

In your niche research, you may find electronics is a best selling niche and you know plenty about it. Remember when I wrote that all the items on my desk would make good products for a Shopify store *except for my phone?* Here's why. The electronics niche is too saturated. No one is going to buy an I-phone or Android from your store. Not only are those items trademarked, no one would ever find you in such a competitive market.

To make the following point, though, I'll use a cell phone as an example. Let's imagine electronics is the best niche for beginning dropshippers. Alas, you have no interest or expertise in electronics. Your expertise ends with the purchase of your last phone. You don't care about buying the latest device the moment it hits the market. You hate researching the topic. You buy whatever tablet the kid next door tells you to buy. You don't know what's hot, and you care even less. The whole subject bores you, and you resent spending so much money on something that will be outdated by the time you take it out of the package.

If this describes you, opening an electronics Shopify store is not a good match. You won't enjoy the process. You might even begin to miss the job you quit in order to start dropshipping. Not only that, how can you convince customers to buy a product you hate or don't care about?

On the flip side, you may love electronics. You love staying abreast of the latest gadgets and you want to own it the instant it hits the market, regardless of the price or the length of the line you have to stand in to get it. But your research proves this is the most saturated, competitive market going.

Don't build a store around something you don't enjoy or understand, and I vehemently recommend you not start a store in a niche where you have virtually no hope of getting noticed.

Both are losing propositions.

Attracting attention to your online store in what you'll spend most of your time doing.

Electronics or gaming or health and fitness are a few of the hardest niches for a beginner to get noticed. Avoid these. At least in the beginning.

Look again at your list and circle some of the items in which you have interest and experience. You don't need to be an expert by any means, but you don't want to hate it either.

General or Niche

Looking at your lists, you should have a few possible niches in which to get started. Before going any farther, you need to decide if you want to build a general store or a niche store.

The difference in the two is exactly what you think it is. A niche store focuses on one category of products while a general store sells items that are typically related, but sometimes not at all.

Think of the old Claire's Boutique stores that were in every shopping mall and sold jewelry and accessories, sunglasses, beach towels, tote bags, and similar items.

A general store is a good option if you aren't ready to settle on one niche. You can use your store to test products and see which ones take off and which ones are dead in the water.

Makes perfect sense, and some experts recommend beginning with a general store because you can test multiple items quickly.

I, however, do not recommend a general store. The market has gotten very competitive, and you should start working to build your brand from the word GO. That will be harder to do with a general store.

You may wonder what exactly is a brand and why you need to build one.

We'll discuss brands further later in this book and in future books in the *Ecommerce Lifestyle* series.

For now, just understand branding is how you'll establish a reputation with your customers. You want them to know what to expect when they visit your store.

If you drove past a store with a sign out front that read: *Dave's*, you wouldn't have a clue what to expect inside. You'd probably keep driving. If the sign read: *Dave's World Famous Oysters on the Half Shell*, you'd have a lot better idea what you were in for when you went inside. You could make an educated decision whether or not you were interested in how world famous Dave's oysters were.

If you plan to take dropshipping seriously—or any ecommerce business—brand-ing will get more important the farther along you go.

That's why I prefer niche stores over general.

Niches build riches.

A niche store focuses on one category of items. Not only is it more easily recognizable for customers who want to know at a glance what you're all about, I believe it looks more professional. You want to earn the customer's trust so they are confident shopping with you. How can you do that if you sell everything from bathing suits to calendars to makeup?

Niche stores that focus on one thing also look high end. Think of your last trip to a mall. (Do they even have those anymore?) But let's pretend. You might see a pipe and tobacco store next to an upscale clothing store. Next to that a fragrance store. The next store selling high end handbags.

There are plenty of stores that sell all these items under one roof. I shop there myself. They make billions of dollars every year and trade well in the stock market. I know what to expect when I walk into these stores. I can buy throw pillows for the family room, treats for my rescue dog, towels for the guest room, and office supplies. One stop shopping certainly makes life easy.

But it can also be confusing for the shopper who doesn't yet know what your store is about. More importantly, it's difficult for the storeowner to promote so many different items. When you are advertising or buying ads, how will you promote your store if you're selling so many different items you don't know where to put your focus?

Again, nothing wrong with it if that's how you choose to run your business. General stores can often earn more revenue and scale up faster because of the ability to test more products, but they have lower conversion rates than niche stores. Investigate all angles before making your decision.

It's all about what you know

If you are focused on fewer items in a specific category, you tend to know more about the products in a niche store. It's easier to efficiently focus your ads. A jewelry store can more easily target ads to a specific market than a store that sells high end pendants and skin care products.

Designing a website for a niche store is also easier and definitely more fun.

For a jewelry store, you can find beautiful stock free photos online to give your store an upscale look. They don't have to just be pictures of the jewelry either. You can use a picture of Big Ben or the Eiffel Tower or the Champs Elysees for your background or header images.

If your store sells saddles, a stock free photo of wild horses running across a range would make a beautiful header image. If you host a blog on your Shopify store site, which I highly recommend and will talk more about in future books, these pictures are easy to find and can inspire blog posts that will hopefully inspire customers to click BUY.

All this drives traffic, helps target customers, and builds your brand.

However you decide to build your store, put yourself in the customer's shoes. Marketers spend bazillions of dollars doing this when designing brick and mortar stores. It's all about the customer and what they expect when they click on an ad linking them to your store.

I'm not suggesting you can't sell saddles *and* jewelry *and* kitchen gadgets. I just wouldn't do them all at once, and definitely not in the beginning. Have you ever heard the old adage: *If you chase two rabbits, they both get away?*

So true. Do your research to figure out which one is the best niche for you to start with and build the best saddle or jewelry or kitchen gadget store you can.

You won't have to stick with one niche the rest of your life. Most successful dropshippers have many stores.

After your leather goods store is earning revenue, and you have the time and knowledge to niche up, start a jewelry store if you want. The key with dropshipping is to start simple. Dropshipping may seem like a huge learning curve for you already. Don't make this harder on yourself. Start with what you know and what you love. Your passion will make success and scaling up faster and easier.

Chapter Three

Solve a Problem

We've talked a lot about niches that are of interest to you, and the importance of enjoying what you do, as well as knowing a little about the niche you create your store in.

Now let's cover the actual research that goes into choosing a successful niche. Look back at the 3 lists you created of items you've purchased and gifts you've bought in the last thirty days. If something is on one of those lists, we know you have an interest in the item, and hopefully a little bit of knowledge.

Now we'll figure out which of these items will make a good niche for you to build a Shopify store.

The key to building a profitable Shopify store is to create it around something people are passionate about. Shopify stores are where people often make impulsive buys. A unique and fun item that catches their eye, and they must have it.

Items that fulfill a want rather than a need are good items to explore. When a person runs out of diapers or mouthwash or a can opener for their camper, they'll stop at the store on their way home from work or order with Amazon Prime and have it delivered in less than an hour. You can't compete with that so don't even try.

What are possible niches that inspire impulse buying? Hobbies is a great place to start. People aren't afraid to spend money on a passion or hobby. A person might quibble for hours over the cost of getting her air conditioner repaired—something she desperately needs—but she won't pause for a moment before dropping $200 on a cute handbag.

I know because I've done it and didn't think twice.

Someone may raise the roof over the cost to fill their tank at the gas station. Yet they won't raise an eyebrow over spending ten times that amount at the golf course next weekend.

We want what we want.

Handing over the equivalent of an entire paycheck to the person fixing our furnace sucks. But spending the same amount for a weekend getaway is fun, and we'll do it again as soon as we have the chance.

Your Shopify store should focus on what people *want* to spend money on, not what they *have* to spend money on.

Look at your list and circle all the items people are passionate about or things they build hobbies around. I'm sure there are several.

You may not be passionate about some of the items on your list, but a significant number of shoppers will be.

Consider makeup or skin care products. Many women are passionate about the products they put on their bodies. They are willing to loosen their purse strings if the product makes them feel younger, more beautiful, thinner, healthier, or just good overall. Many will spend twice the price that it costs at a big box store if the product claims to protect the environment or the inhabitants of it.

People who are passionate about a sport or their yard or property, their cars, pets, or a hobby are potential customers for your Shopify store if you provide the right product.

People such as golfers. Fishermen. Crafters. Car enthusiasts. Gardeners and backyard landscapers. Pet owners. Parents.

Think about gadgets or kitchen accessories. A niche that would fit both categories is a good niche to consider. You can open a can of beans with a military style P-38. It is a manual can opener with a hinged blade that opens cans in the field. Soldiers used to wear them on a chain around their necks with their dog tags. A person can avoid starvation with nothing more than a P-38. It isn't pretty or comfortable or convenient, but it does what it's supposed to do. However, very few kitchens are equipped with them.

People are passionate about stocking their homes with the latest gadgets and conveniences. Any niche that appeals to that passion is a good choice to build a store around.

Things like pretty pillows for the sofa. Customers tire of the ones they have and your store sells beautiful ones with modern motifs. Maybe your customer saw a kitchen gadget at a friend's house and realized she couldn't live without it. The gadget solved a problem, filled a need, was cool and trendy, so she ordered it right then on her phone.

Imagine a customer who loves dolphins or penguins or koala bears or English Springer Spaniels. He or she would go crazy over a dolphin cell phone case. Cell phone cases are typically not a good niche, but a dolphin cell phone case would be unique and interesting to a person who is passionate about dolphins. Something they've never seen before that feeds their passion.

A niche that encourages upselling with related items is tailor made for dropshipping. If you've decided to sell kitchen gadgets, you can carry additional items customers will buy to accentuate their original purchase. If they buy a set of steak knives, you can upsell to them by offering cooking knives, a knife rack, and a chopping block.

When choosing a niche, ask yourself how it works with bundling items. Create a product bundle with items like a diaper bag and a matching car seat cover. Increase the size of the bundle with a few more items that make travel with baby fun and easy. Create a better price if customers buy all related items. You may take a 20% loss on the car seat cover, but customers will be encouraged to buy more items than they originally intended so you still earn more with the overall purchase.

Bundling is a very successful method of upselling.

No one can resist a bargain, even if it ultimately means they spend more.

There are apps that help with this we'll discuss at length in future books. You may have fallen prey to these tactics yourself. I'm sure you've noticed the *Also Bought* items strategically placed under the product description of something you're shopping for on Amazon or the *Similar Items* listings on Ebay. They're not there by mistake.

When you buy something or even look at an item, an app will suggest you might also like a related item. Apps like this help convert sales, encourage upselling, and tempt a customer to add the additional item to their cart, even if they're not ready to buy.

To recap, when choosing an item to sell in your Shopify store, you have a better chance of finding a winner if it fits into one or more of the following categories.

- People are passionate about it.
- Trending items or items a person buys more than one of.
- A unique product the customer won't find at the local Target store.
- An impulse buy item.

Now that you have some ideas of potential niches and products, you need to research to see if there is a market to sustain them. There are many different ways to do this that don't involve buying additional programs and software unless you want to. My first suggestion is using Google Trends. This is a great research tool and totally free for you to use.

Go there and type in a search term in the search box at the top of the page. Google Trends will show you a graph of interest over time. As an example, I typed in hummingbird feeders. Where I live in the middle of the United States, people are crazy over hummingbirds. Not surprisingly, from September through the last week of March, the searches for feeders were pretty low. But beginning at the end of March through the summer months, results were at nearly 100%.

Also as expected, the United States showed the biggest interest in hummingbird feeders by region, which is the next chart you'll see on Google Trends. Canada was a close second, while it doesn't look like the rest of the world cares a whole heck of a lot about hummingbirds.

This information will help you target your ads to the U.S. and Canada.

You may not want to go with seasonal items for your first few products, but it's totally up to you. If you decide to carry hummingbird feeders in your Shopify store, don't wait until

June 1st to start promoting them. Most avid birdwatchers are expecting the little guys by the first of April or even sooner depending on where they live, and they want their yards and porches equipped in time for the hummingbirds' arrival.

After seeing how an item is trending, I check out Aliexpress, which is the distributor where most dropshippers get their products.

When you start typing a word into the search box on Aliexpress, you will see a drop down list of similar results that others have searched for and the number of searches for each. This will show you how big of a market is out there for your product

While looking for hummingbird feeders, I typed in *humming* and then paused. A drop down list showed me what other shoppers searched for when beginning with the word *humming*. The results included hummingbird jewelry, tattoos, feeders, and feeder cleaners, among others.

You may be all set to sell hummingbird feeders, and your research proves it will make a profitable niche. As you dig deeper into that same niche, you may realize other products will sell even better. Your store may rank too low to get noticed for hummingbird feeders, but you may easily get to Page One of the search engine results under hummingbird tattoos.

Research is paramount. Don't stop at the first possibility. Keep digging. You could very well strike gold.

Chapter Four

What to sell and where to get it

You've researched niches that encourage impulse shopping by buyers passionate about specific products and who are willing to spend money at your store. You researched Aliexpress bestsellers. You chose a niche that isn't over-saturated and in which you have some interest or expertise.

Now it's time to select products to sell on your Shopify store.

I've put this chapter before setting up your Shopify store simply because you need products to sell before you build a store in which to sell them. As I mentioned earlier, your free Shopify trial begins the instant you set up your account. You want to complete as much work and research possible before you get to this step. Your 14-day trial should be used for setting up your store and making money. I don't want you to waste a moment doing anything else.

For me, this part of the process is the most fun in creating a Shopify store.

You are creating a store from the ground up. Everything is brand new. Think of walking into a new house or the first time you get behind the wheel of a brand new car at a dealership. You can't deny the rush of excitement in your belly.

It's the same with your store. Endless potential.

Have fun stocking your store. Go back to Google Trends and Aliexpress and type in possible products or items you want to investigate. Again, the first possibility might not be the best one.

Amazon and Ebay are also great places for research. They have the same drop down boxes that give you ideas about related products that are selling well. If you're considering a popular category like pets or health and beauty or baby, niche down to find a specific product that isn't being sold to death in every Shopify store out there.

Don't feel like you need to rush the process. However, don't let this step cripple you either. Sometimes we're so worried we'll make the wrong decision we don't do anything. Thousands of visitors go to the Shopify website every day, yet never set up an account or do anything beyond seeing what it's all about.

There is money to be made in dropshipping. The opportunity is there. The capability is there, but many potential drop-shippers let fear of failure stop them from even trying.

You can't open your store and start earning revenue unless you act.

You can't open your store and start earning revenue unless you act. Even a wrong decision is betterthan no decision at all.

♦♦♦

Once you've chosen the items to sell in your store, you need to decide which supplier to use to dropship those products to your customers. The most used is Aliexpress. Aliexpress is an online retail service made up of businesses mostly in China that facilitates sales to customers all over the world. When a customer clicks BUY on an item in your store, the order will probably be filled by an Aliexpress supplier.

There are other sites where you can find dropshipping products like Wish.com, but for this book we'll focus on Aliexpress. Just note it isn't your only option. Nor should it be the only one you consider when ordering products.

There are several things you need to know before linking your store to Aliexpress or another distributor. First of all, most items will come from China. Most customers expect this, but others take pride in ordering items *not* made in China. Make sure customers know you are not creating these items in your basement. You shouldn't make a big deal of pointing out items are made in China or another country, but you don't want to mislead customers either.

Secondly, shipping will take longer than the usual 5-7 days it takes to get something from Amazon or Ebay. Earlier I wrote that you can't compete with Amazon Prime. You mustn't even try. You are not selling convenience here. You are selling unique products and a unique shopping experience. Just make sure you don't

CAITLYN RICH - *63*

hide this from customers or hope they won't notice the tiny disclaimer on your site.

I recently ordered three unrelated items from Aliexpress to see how close to the posted shipping times they came. Two items arrived within 3 weeks, which is what I expected. I'm not an impatient person, and I knew this when I placed the order. The third item took 26 days from the date I received an email from the supplier letting me know the item had been shipped. Altogether it took 33 days for me to receive it.

The shipper guaranteed delivery within 60 days. That's a long time, even for the most patient customer. Personally, I wouldn't carry an item in my store that could take up to 60 days for delivery. Most customers won't want to wait that long unless they're in prison for a major crime and 60 days is a drop in the bucket on their calendar. If you choose to stock these items in your store, be honest and upfront with customers.

Quality customer service dictates the customer receives an email the day the item ships. (The only supplier to send this notification was the one that took the longest for me to receive my item. There are apps that automatically do this so you won't have to stay on top of it yourself.) If your customer has not received their order after 14 days or so, schedule an email thanking them for their patience and assuring them the item is on its way. The day the item arrives, they should receive another email thanking them for their purchase, and you hope they love it and it meets their expectations.

Again, an app will do this for you once you create an email for each situation and schedule them to arrive emails as warranted.

When deciding which distributors to use to stock your Shopify store, determining estimated shipping times is very important. Most items I stock take 20-30 days to receive. Even 30 days is a long time for customers who are used to having orders filled in an hour.

You may sell a product customers are willing to wait for. Let them decide, not you.

Whatever the time frame, be transparent. Let customers know if the item's expected delivery is six days or six weeks. Be honest. Be patient and sympathetic. Be understanding when they take their frustration out on you even though you did everything you could to make them aware of shipping estimates. Some will complain after they haven't received their products in three days. You will get cancellation requests. You will get bad reviews. You will get nasty emails from customers wanting to know where's their stuff.

Always be understanding and courteous, even when you're right and the customer's a horse's behind. Stay in contact. As soon as you get a tracking number for the order, email it to the buyer. Thank them for their patience and their business, even if they aren't patient and you hope you never hear from them again.

I send 3 emails to customers after they receive their order. One when the item is delivered. Then 2 days later and another one 7 days later. In these emails, I thank them for their business, ask how they are enjoying the product, and if they would leave a review. Good reviews are super important, as you'll discover once you open your store.

Stock quality products and provide good customer service and don't hesitate to ask for reviews. You will get negative reviews, so don't freak out when it happens. You can respond privately if you choose, but never allow the customer to bait you into an argument. Even when they're wrong, you will always come out the loser. Not only that, life is short, and there are some people you just can't please. Provide the best service possible and move on.

The last chapter of this book contains three free apps to include in your Shopify store that will automate much of your customer service tasks for you. Once you personalize each email unique to your store, they'll be on autopilot and you won't have to give them much thought hereafter.

Have you ever bought something but didn't open the package or use it for a week? Your customers are busy. They'll do the same thing sometimes, even after they whine about how long it took the item to arrive. Don't expect them to fall in love with your product the same day and tell their friends about it on social media. When you contact your customers, make sure it isn't only to ask them to do something for you. Every contact should be about the customer's needs. Your needs are always secondary.

♦♦♦

As important as it is to stay in touch with customers, it is equally important to stay in touch with your distributors. If there is a delay in your customer getting their purchase, the distributor should let you know. If not, reach out to them. Before you begin business with them, find out their policy about an item that arrives damaged or never arrives at all.

As the storeowner, you bear the responsibility for this with the customer. There are other things that go wrong with orders. The distributor won't care nearly as much as you will. Their only concern is to move items from their warehouses to the customer. When things go wrong—and they certainly will—it will rest on your shoulders. Accept it now. That's why dropshipping is a simple method of making money, but it isn't easy.

Before an item is shipped you will need to make arrangements with the distributor that the invoice bears your store name and not the name of the supplier. You don't want to point out to the customer they could've ordered the item directly from the supplier and avoided your markup. You are not being dishonest by not divulging this information. Most buyers only care about receiving their product, not the details or the process of doing so.

If they had done a little research, they would've already known this anyway.

If you are in the United States you may want to look into selling products from American distributors. Shipping is much faster from a domestic distributor, and some customers are proud to support an American business. Of course, items will cost more, and you will have to pass this expense onto your customers.

If your demographic is upscale shoppers who care less about price than they do about receiving unique, high quality items, this won't matter. Do your research. Only you can know if you want to find an American company. Currently, the biggest online retail market is inside the U.S., though your products will be available worldwide. American made products may sell better to your target audience than a less expensive version. All this depends on your product and how you market it. It is certainly something to consider.

You can also have items created with your own private label on them. Instead of selling a generic cake pan, you can have a supplier create a pan or set of pans bearing your company logo. How fun is that! Private labeling a product will increase the price, but it will also increase your salability. Customers trust a product more with a private label than one without.

Private labeling isn't a difficult process. It just takes research to make sure the item is a winning product people are willing to spend more on.

Much of this depends on what type of Shopify store you wish to build. You may know of a locally made product you believe you can sell in your store. Meet directly with the manufacturer and see what sort of deal you can agree to. Local businesses can offer unique, upscale items customers won't find anywhere else, and they'll be proud to see a Made in USA label.

I live in an area with a large Amish and Mennonite population. Local cottage industries are huge employers here and sell everything from furniture to personalized iron door hangers to cabinets to fireplace inserts, all crafted by Amish or Mennonite businesses.

These products carry a heftier price tag than similar, mass-produced items at our local home improvement stores. Yet these businesses have no shortage of orders. In fact, they are growing at amazing rates. When selling from a local manufacturer, your shipping rates and tax rates will be a completely different ballgame than the usual free shipping you get from Aliexpress.

Consider your product choice from all angles when deciding how to run your store. Which brings us to the chapter you've been anticipating, Setting up your Shopify Store.

Chapter Five

Setting up Your Shopify Store

I'm not going to waste space here with step -by-step instructions on how to open a Shopify account and set up your store. Shopity will walk you through the process when you go to their site. What I will tell you are things to keep in mind when doing so.

Shopify has many different templates available to set up your store. Begin with a free one. You can upgrade once your store is earning revenue. You don't want to over think this process. The more time you spend at this is time you could be selling products.

All you need to remember is Simplicity scores over Complexity.

Many potential dropshippers spend weeks setting up their stores. They agonize over every little detail and worry one product description or one poorly chosen graphic will knock them out of business. Don't let this be you. Every day you don't have your store up and running is a day you could be earning revenue.

Decide what kind of store you want to open and get the store selling. You will never run out of features or apps to install that improve your store's performance or make it trendy or cool. An app that tells visitors *Jocelyn K. from Wichita, KS* just purchased the item they are considering is fun to watch and gives the store credibility. Just don't put off selling because you don't know how to activate the app or what font to use.

Don't delay opening your store because you can't decide if your BUY button should be orange or green. Get to selling.

You'll have plenty of time to upgrade and reinvest money into your store after you are earning revenue. You can reinvest your profits once you have some.

After you are making money, you can upgrade to a paid template with more features if you want. Don't worry about it in the beginning. The most important things going in is having a product to sell and capturing emails of visitors so you can promote to them in the future.

I recommend new storeowners stock five to ten related items in their stores. It isn't necessary to wait until you have ten guaranteed bestsellers before you open for business. Start with one. Open your store, and then add the other items.

Just get started.

Personalization

There are thousands of online stores, many of which sell the same products your store will sell. You need to stand out.

In order to do that right away is to personalize your website. Do not use the free website that comes with your Shopify account, even on Day One. You do not want your store name to be My Amazing Store dot Shopify dot com.

Nothing looks more amateurish or illegitimate.

It is inconceivable for any business to try to survive—let alone stand out from the competition—in today's ecommerce climate without a web presence. You want customers to remember you. You want them to take you seriously. You want them to trust you. Shopify can't do this for you.

Everything is in the name. While choosing your niche and building your brand, keep this in mind. Once you choose a name for your store, find a web host and buy the domain. You don't need to learn web design or hire a developer to have an interesting, interactive site. A good host company will do most of the work for you. There are several that charge about $12 a year to host your domain, so there's no reason you can't afford it.

If your store sells automotive accessories and you want to call the store *Enigma Automotive Supplies* make sure the name is available. If it's already taken, choose a new name or consider a logical, easy to remember variation. You don't want a convoluted web name that no one can remember or pronounce. Don't name your site Enigma, underscore, hash tag Automotive 3-4-0 just to get the domain name. Don't get cute with spelling or phonetics. It's annoying, and people will still forget you.

To create an engaging store and interesting shopping experience, you need images. Not just images of your products. Adding pictures—and even video—to your store is easy, and you probably already know how. The main thing is to compress your images so they don't slow down your page load times. There are plenty of programs that do this for you or you can play around with them yourself. However you decide to work with images, make sure to test their appearance so you can see how they look across all devices.

Most shoppers will access your site on a mobile device so make sure it is readable, clear, and easy to navigate. The last thing you want to do is put so much work into creating a store, only to have the lion's share of your customers frustrated by how poorly it shows up on their devices.

If you have no idea how to start, go to YouTube and search for tutorials that will make setting up your website simple and fast.

About Us Page

Besides products to sell, appealing images, and a contact page, the only other page you should set up right away in your *About Us* page. You are building trust here. You want store visitors to know you aren't a fake company trying to steal their identity.

Your store should be as unique as you are. Just the fact that you go to the trouble to create a unique *About Us* page will set you apart from other dropshippers. Many stores don't bother. Beginning dropshippers are intimidated by this step and don't know where to begin so they don't do anything. They figure most people don't read the *About Us* page, and anything on it will be fabricated or wildly embellished since they've only been in business since Tuesday. Both points may be true, but it's an important step for several reasons.

Even though many visitors won't read your *About Us* page, it gives your company a look of credibility and professionalism. In fact, a store without an *About Us* page screams *dropshipper*. You don't want to advertise that you're a middleman, and the customer could go directly to your supplier and get the same product for less money.

You want your site to assure potential customers the only way to get this amazing and unique product they won't find on the shelf at their local T.J. Maxx is by doing business with you.

"What if I don't have anything to say?" you may wonder. *"I started my business yesterday and I have no logical explanation about why I'm selling flowerpots."*

Not to worry.

Instead of focusing on your lack of experience when writing your *About Us* page, focus on your desire to solve your customers' problems. That's what they care about anyway. Focus on why you're different, even if you're selling the same product as your competitors. You don't have to write your life story. You don't need to explain your motivation about why you're selling flowerpots or how much dirt means to you. The only thing the reader cares about is how it applies to them.

This is your story. It shouldn't be that difficult to put into a few words what makes your customer relate to you. Remember, the store is about the customer and filling their need or solving their problem. You want them to understand how your store is equipped to do exactly that.

Consider something like this:

Here at Sunshine Gardens *we take pride in offering beauty and convenience at a reasonable price. Just like you, we want our living spaces to be reflections of who we are and what matters most to us. Our flowerpots are durable and beautiful, two things we all look for when planning our outdoor space. Browse our inventory and we're confident you'll find a unique piece that fits your vision of the ultimate backyard oasis. Contact us anytime with questions or suggestions on how we can improve your shopping experience and what products you would like* Sunshine Gardens *to bring to you in the future. As always, we appreciate your time and business. If you have a few moments, please leave an honest review to help other customers know what we're about.*

That's it. Add your contact info, top it off with a beautiful header picture that suits the theme of your store, and you've created a unique *About Us* page that will set you apart from other beginning dropshippers. You even gently reminded them to leave a review.

Descriptions that Sell

No matter how bad you think you are at describing something, you must describe your product to customers in a way that makes it impossible for them to leave your store without making a purchase.

You cannot rely on the default sales description that came from the supplier to do it for you. Go to Aliexpress right now and look up a few random products. I dare you not to cringe at the descriptions. Not only will those descriptions be the same as on every other online store that stocks the products, they are horrible.

You don't have to be an English major to see what doesn't work. Incomplete sentences. Incorrect pronouns or syntax. Descriptions that don't adequately describe the product you so carefully chose. Worst of all, they don't even mention the product's benefits.

I'm not suggesting your descriptions

should be English major grade writing. Write the way your customers talk. Incomplete sentences are fine if they convey a point in a succinct and interesting way. I'm sure you noticed plenty of them already in this book.

By no means should you copy and paste the descriptions from your supplier. There will be other dropshippers who do this, and you want to set your store apart from them.

Product description should focus on the benefits of the product, not the features.

What's the difference? you may ask.

First of all, let me assure you it is much easier to market a product's benefits than its features.

As a new storeowner, you should start seeing yourself as a problem solver instead of a product seller.

This is what I mean:

You are selling a product, but the only thing your customer cares about is how said product solves their problem. People care about the benefits of a product. Even the least selfish among us often ask: *What's in it for me?*

Consider a product as simple as facial scrub. What features of a facial scrub would make you select it above all other facial scrubs? The pretty packaging? The fresh scent? The creamy texture? The little granules that exfoliate as it cleanses?

Probably all of the above.

Those features are great, but they're hard to sell. A customer visiting your dropshipping store can't smell the fresh apricot scent. They can't feel the creamy texture or the exfoliating granules. Focus instead on the benefits, which they can understand.

What problem does a facial scrub solve? It cleans your face. It exfoliates. It leaves skin luminous and reduces pores. It brightens and tightens.

Benefits convert more sales than features.

When writing a product description for your amazing product, expound on those benefits.

How do those little granules benefit your skin? They energize the skin, making it feel softer and younger. They turn back the clock. They fight aging.

How could that not sell?

That example may be pretty obvious. Selling the benefits of facial scrub is easy. What if you're selling a fidget spinner, which of course you won't since that ship has sailed and we all missed it. You may not be able to think of one benefit of a fidget spinner. It doesn't solve a problem. It won't change the world. It won't cure cancer. It won't save a person's marriage.

The benefits? you ask. There aren't any, except it keeps the kids occupied.

It might not fix a huge problem, but even a fidget spinner has benefits. It's fun. It's a stress reliever. It can be an icebreaker. It's a low cost item and simple to use. You can share it with friends and compete against each other. It solves a problem even if the benefits won't change the world.

Get Specific

When writing your descriptions, use keywords to get attention to your store and products. Keywords are words or phrases people type into search engines to find products or information they want. If you type *gardening* or *flowers* into a search engine, you will get a bazillion results—too many to help potential customers find you. Instead, find a word or phrase with fewer results that will help customers zero in on your beautiful flowerpots.

Keywords shouldn't be too competitive so no one finds you. Nor should they be so narrow that no one is even searching for that keyword.

A Google search will reveal all sorts of keyword search tools that show how many times a word or phrase is typed into a search engine. I prefer doing it myself, especially in the beginning when you are on a budget. Look for either free keyword search tools online or do some related searches yourself.

We know without looking the word *flowerpot* will have too many results, and a customer won't find you until Page 50. No one goes to

Page 50. Fewer than 10% of browsers scroll past Page One. Instead, try using longer tail keywords like *terra cotta pots, decorative terra cotta pots,* or *terra cotta clay pots* that are more likely to help you rank higher in the search engines.

Google, Bing, and even Amazon or Ebay search engines help with this process. Type one or two words into the search box and pause. The same drop down list you used when looking for niches and products will reveal long tail keyword searches your potential customers are looking for. Click on different ones that fit your product and see what the rankings are. A high number means plenty of people are looking for that product. Too low means no one wants it. Choose a keyword or phrase somewhere in the middle. Make a list. You will be tweaking and adjusting this as long as you're selling this product. Few of us land on the perfect keyword the first time.

Don't let this step stymie you and keep you from moving forward with your dropshipping business.

Email

In all the things necessary for setting up a successful Shopify store, the most important element is arguably collecting email. The difference in businesses that do okay and those that are wildly successful is the capturing of email addresses. Without email addresses of customers and browsers, how will you tempt them to come back and buy again or complete the order they didn't finish the first time? How will you know who to target with future ads or promotions? How will you let them know of a sale or new product?

You must collect emails. This is the one thing you must set up before taking your store Live. Do not skip this step.

Good news. It's not that hard, and it's free. At least in the beginning. I have included more details in the last chapter about setting up an app that collects email addresses for you, so I'll save that information for then.

Just know collecting emails is the lifeblood of your business and must not be overlooked if you want to be successful now and in the future.

Chapter Six

Running Your Business, Day to Day

You researched and selected a niche in which you can stand out while selling products customers want. You stocked your store with products your customers will be excited to buy.

Once you set up your Shopify account and choose a template that's easy for customers to navigate, you can place a few Facebook ads and get some influencers on Instagram. After that, you can sit back and watch those orders pour in. Right?

Couldn't be further from the truth.

90% of Shopify stores fail because many hopeful dropshippers believe exactly that. This system is simple, but it's not easy money just waiting to pour into your bank account.

If you want to succeed at dropshipping, you must respect your business and work it every single day.

Imagine pulling into your usual gas station tomorrow morning to fill up your tank before work, and the place is closed. The doors are locked. The lights are off. No explanation as far as you can tell, just deserted.

You drive by the next morning, and there they are, bright and early, open for business. Curious, you go inside and ask what happened the day before. The clerk behind the counter says; "Oh, nothing happened. We just decided not to work. We were up late the night before and the kids were sick and we had guests from out of town. We didn't feel like opening up."

A month later the same thing happens again, only they don't offer an explanation this time. They just don't feel like working. If someone were to actually run a business like this, it wouldn't be long before that gas station began to lose customers. There are plenty of places to buy gas. Why bother with one you can't depend on to be there when you need them?

Many online entrepreneurs believe they

can work their business whenever they feel like it or have a few extra hours in their schedule, and they'll still succeed. They're busy during the week so they'll double down on the weekend. Their daughter is getting married, so they'll hit it really hard after the wedding.

If you don't develop a winning mindset and determine to treat your dropshipping business like a business, you will be one of the 90% of Shopify stores that fail. There is money to be made in dropshipping. Lots of it. Enough for every diligent dropshipper out there. But you must work your business with the same drive and discipline as you would if you operated a landscaping business or bakery or manufacturing plant.

If you want to scale up your business to making hundreds—and even thousands of dollars a day—you must work the business and be here for the long haul.

I'll only mention the 80/20 rule here because it applies. You've probably heard it a dozen other places already. You will spend 80% of your time doing stuff that nets 20% of your profits. Watch how you spend your time. If you're going to spend an entire weekend installing one cool app you think everyone else has, and that feature only ups your sales by one tenth of a percent, I can guarantee you should've spent your weekend doing something more beneficial to your business.

Ads

You set up your store and write amazing product descriptions and post beautiful high quality pictures. But no one knows you exist. The only way to let them know is by placing ads. Since we hope to get into dropshipping with the lowest threshold possible, don't try to reinvent the wheel. You needn't search for unique ways to reach customers.

Every dropshipper needs to harness the power of online marketing if they hope to be successful. It's so easy now to advertise to millions of people around the world without breaking the bank. You don't need to try to sell your product to the entire world. Most of the world isn't interested in your terra cotta clay pots or fidget spinners or whatever it is you're selling. But there are enough shoppers who are, and once you learn where to find them, you'll see your sales skyrocket.

There is no one size fits all method to placing ads. For the sake of this book, I'm only going to talk about Facebook ads. With 1.8 billion active monthly users, Facebook will surely have a huge reach to your targeted customers. The ads are simple to place. There is a plan to suit any budget that will appeal to any demographic.

Marketers love Facebook ads because of how specific you can target them. Facebook collects detailed and unique information from its users for you. If you want to target women aged 30-60 who love to garden and would be interested in your terra cotta pots, you can search hobby and interest groups on Facebook to find them.

Simply go to the Ads Manager page on Facebook. Choose an objective for the ad you want to create. I usually select *Purchase Objective* since the primary goal of an ad is to get visitors to make a purchase. There are different objectives for ads like *Add to Cart* or *Website Visits*. You can certainly explore those further and find what works best for your store or the situation.

After you choose the objective for your ad, select your audience. You want to reach as broad an audience as possible. If you are selling a water bottle, you will target groups that have expressed an interest in similar products. Runners would be a logical choice. But don't stop there. Go broad. Pet owners carry water for their four-legged friends. Parents, bikers, tourists, people with long commutes—all these groups could use your product.

Don't stop thinking as soon as you reach the most obvious conclusion or you will be leaving money on the table.

Remember you are solving a problem, not just selling a product. Figure out how you can solve the problem of people in the biggest target groups possible and focus your ads accordingly.

Be mindful that Facebook is constantly updating their ad placement policies. Most changes won't directly affect the ads you hope to place, but don't be surprised if something comes along that does.

Customer Service

In dropshipping, as in every other industry, customer is King. You'd never know it with many dropshipping businesses. Many of them are run with the goal of selling the most products at the highest price without a lot of concern about customer satisfaction.

Big mistake. If you want to build a lasting brand, how you treat your customers and how they think of you should be your second greatest concern after giving them the best products possible to solve their problem. Some dropshippers who don't care about their customers may make money initially. But turning your back on the customers you rely on will never end well.

With everything you do in your dropshipping business, you must keep the customer in mind. The first time a customer comes to your store, their biggest concern is credibility. Are you real or not? Are you going to scam them? Are you another unsecured site selling imaginary products they'll never receive?

Providing excellent customer service will go a long way in assuring customers they are safe in your hands. Make it easy for them to connect with you. Let them know you share their passions. You understand their needs. Build trust so they know they can safely and securely buy from your store.

Answer questions in a timely manner. There are apps to help with this, but you don't need a bunch of them to get started. Waiting until the store is perfect with fun and amazing apps, a fancy template, and twenty-five products to sell will only slow you down and keep you from enriching customers' lives with products that solve their problems.

Be patient. Be credible. Be respectful. Treat customers' the way you want to be treated anytime you go online or walk into an actual store.

Never stop working

The only guarantee you'll get in anything is you are sure to fail if you never take action.

The main objective for many of us hoping

to succeed in an ecommerce business is to break away from the job that currently enslaves us. We want to free up time to do what we really want. To spend it with those who matter most.

One thing is certain in dropshipping: success won't come if you don't work your plan. Or test your products and test your ads. Or ask customers what they want and what you can do to improve.

Maybe you only have one item for sale in your store today. You don't need anything more than that to start. One product that solves one problem.

Don't be afraid to change. Be willing to admit you may have missed something along the way. If your products aren't selling or no one is finding your store, look objectively at every element of your business. Maybe your ad stinks. Maybe you don't have a good product. Maybe your price is too high. Or too low. Yes, that happens too.

Test. Test. Test.

Test your keywords. Test your background images and headers and product descriptions.

Test your ads. Test products. Your first product may not be a winner. Your tenth product isn't selling either.

You did the research. It was trending when you looked at it, but a week later you couldn't give it away. Don't give up because one item doesn't sell, or you didn't make money in your first ninety days. As with any business, you need patience, perseverance, and hard work.

Find another product. And then another. Write another ad. Give your dropshipping business a chance the same way you would if you opened a restaurant and it took some time to get customers in the door to try your food.

It's amazing how many people never accomplish anything because they refuse to start. They put off opening their store because everything isn't perfect. They tell themselves as soon as they get one more element in place, complete one more task, add one more app, they'll open their store.

Often that time never comes. Don't get caught in this trap. You don't have to do everything you think every other dropshipper is doing. Every day that goes by you are not listing and selling products is another day you're not making money.

> *"Do not wait; the time will never*
> *be just right. Start where you stand,*
> *and work with whatever tools*
> *you may have at your command,*
> *and better tools will be found*
> *as you go along." ---George Herbert*

Start today. Do something for your business today. Don't wait until the process to get into dropshipping changes and you have to learn a whole new system. Stop waiting. Stop putting off your success.

Make a plan. Follow it. Adjust as you go when you see what works and what doesn't. Do the work, and the money will follow.

Chapter Seven

Top Free Apps Your Store Needs

Congratulations. You have your Shopify store up and running. You have at least one product to sell, and you may already be earning revenue. If not, don't stress. You are successful because you are progressively realizing a worthwhile goal.

For most, success in dropshipping doesn't happen overnight. You are moving in that direction, and that makes you a success already.

The following 3 Free apps are my pick to include on your Shopify store as you begin your dropshipping journey. There are thousands of apps available that perform a myriad of tasks to make running your store easier, more efficient, and more fun. At this point, we won't get bogged down or complicate the process so much that you never start, so I'm only covering three in this book.

At the time of the writing of this book, the following apps were free. I cannot guarantee they still are upon your reading of the book. If they're no longer free, I'll wager they're still worth the money. If you decide they're not, there are plenty of apps that do much the same thing that will cost you nothing, or next to nothing. There are many more apps worth investing in for a minimal amount of money that may pay for themselves with just one sale.

In the beginning, though, we want to keep it as simple—and cheap—as possible.

You may wonder if you need to include apps at all in your store. Doesn't it just mean more work setting up the store when all you really want to do is start selling products?

It may seem that way, but apps make your life easier and perform so many functions you might not think important in the beginning.

Apps build trust with customers and make your store look more legitimate. When customers find your store trustworthy, they are more likely to click BUY. Anything you can do to convert browsers into customers—especially free things—is definitely worth the small amount of effort you put into it today.

Apps help with marketing, which generates more revenue and increases your average order value. They automate tasks that can use up much of your time. When apps automate those time-sucking chores for you, you're free to focus on other elements of the dropshipping business that earn revenue. And that's why we're all here.

As I wrote in Chapter Five, capturing email addresses is imperative to your success. If you do not have an email collection system in place for visitors to your store, you are losing potential revenue you can't get any other way. That's why I'm starting my list with an email automation platform.

Mailchimp

Email addresses of your customers and potential customers are the lifeblood of your dropshipping business. You can do everything right, but if you are not building your email list, you are throwing away money.

Email lists are what differentiate between

stores that are practically printing money & stores that don't do well. You can easily set up your Mailchimp auto-responder so emails go out to shoppers wherever they are in the shopping process.

Mailchimp is the world's largest marketing automation platform. Whether you're letting customers know about a sale or introducing a new product or offering them a special discount because you haven't heard from them in a while, Mailchimp's campaign builder makes it easy to create a marketing campaign to get your message out there.

It has the capability to automatically send an email to a customer, who for whatever reason, abandoned their cart. Whether the phone rang or the dog threw up on the carpet or they fell down a well, you can automatically send them an email reminding them of the great product they might miss out on if they don't come back and complete their order. You can personalize the program to offer customers an incentive to come back and complete their order, such as giving them a percentage off their entire order, or an additional discount if they bundle with another product.

The possibilities are only limited by your imagination.

Mailchimp is free until you've captured 2000 email addresses. After that, it's still affordable. It's a great program for getting started. You do not want to start your store without an app that collects emails so start with Mailchimp.

Oberlo

You want to automate as many aspects of your dropshipping business as soon as possible. You'll have enough to do in the beginning while building your business, and you can't afford to spend time filling orders one at a time. Work smart, not hard. Oberlo helps you do that.

Oberlo is a free app that allows you to fulfill orders via Aliexpress very quickly. Import products directly into your store and ship them to customers in just a few clicks so you don't have to fulfill orders manually. With it, you find the products you want to import, publish them to your store, and start selling directly to customers.

The app autofills your customer's information into Aliexpress and makes the order process much easier for you and your customer. (Don't you love it when websites do it for you?) It keeps track of inventory levels so you never sell an item that's out of stock. It keeps track of changing prices and makes sure what you are charging customers is up to date.

With Oberlo, you can easily edit your product descriptions, change titles, or add new images. You'll never lose track of your orders with integrated order tracking. You can even import only products with the fastest delivery time and switch between suppliers who offer the best price.

Oberlo's starter plan is free until you reach 50 orders a month. By the time you need the Basic plan, your store will be earning more than enough revenue to cover the cost. You may even cover it with just one sale.

Kit

Can you afford a personal assistant? Most

of us can't. But with Kit, another free Shopify app, you can have many benefits of a virtual assistant without paying for one. Kit communicates with you through messaging so it's truly like having a personal assistant.

Kit can handle all your marketing tasks on your Shopify store like setting up Facebook or Instagram ads, including ads that retarget past customers. It can post Facebook updates for you to engage your customers. It can create and promote discount codes for customers who left your store without buying or help to acquire new customers.

Kit generates reports that provide insight on ads and sales performance. While monitoring sales, Kit may recognize some of your products aren't selling as well as they did last month. Kit can orchestrate a sale, verify the amount you're willing to spend, and work out how to promote the sale.

Utilizing Kit allows you to focus on running your store and giving up a lot of the chores you don't want to do anyway. Don't worry, Kit may take over a lot of your tasks, but you're still the boss. Sort of.

There are many other apps you may decide you can't live without. In fact, choosing only 3 to add to your store was nearly impossible for me. Before long you'll come up with your own list of Must-Have's, but 3 is enough to get your store off to a running start.

Conclusion

I've used this phrase before in other situations, but it fits here too.

**Don't focus on perfection,
focus on professionalism.**

Your store may never be perfect. You will continue to find things you wish you had done differently. You'll watch a dropshipping guru's YouTube video and cringe at all the things you did wrong. Or rather, the things you *think* you did wrong.

None of us are perfect, even those gurus who claim to make $20,000 before lunch. If you wait until your store is perfect before going Live, you'll never do it. If I waited until this book was perfect and had covered absolutely every possible aspect of running a dropshipping business, I never would've published it. If I did include everything there is to know about dropshipping in the book, you wouldn't be able to lift it because it would be about 10,000 pages long.

Stop stressing over every minute detail. Make it easy on yourself. Get your store up and running. You can add apps later. You can second guess your font size or your BUY button color anytime. As long as you are providing products customers want that solves a problem for them, they're not going to leave your store over the color of a button.

If the technological aspects of running your dropshipping business intimidate you, hire someone to take over those tasks for you once you're earning revenue. Or have the kid next door explain it.

The best you can do is aim for professionalism, not perfection.

Provide customers with products that enrich their lives and solve a problem.

Be trustworthy and honest and give them the best shopping experience you can.

Do your research. Make your own decisions and move forward. Avoid the naysayers. We have enough of them in every other area of our life. Only we can be responsible for our choices and actions.

Many gurus say to measure success by how much money you make. They encourage you to create goals like this:

- My business will earn $10K a month within 90 days.

- I will make 6 figures by the end of the year.

- By one year from today, I will have earned a million dollars.

Instead, create goals that are completely within your control. Goals like:

- This week I will research and select 10 items to stock in my store.

- Today I will create 5 personalized automatic email responses for my customers.

- Today I will apply for 10 Instagram Influencer shout-outs, even if I think I'll never get them.

- By the end of the week I will place 10 ads on Facebook.

- This month I will enroll in a course on social media marketing.

There's nothing wrong with setting goals for your business, but in the beginning, don't stress over ones that have too many variables. Focus on tasks you can do that help you move forward toward your long term goals and scale up your business faster. The money will follow.

Avoid negativity. I'm sure you have people in your life who are only happy when they're complaining or looking for the bad in any situation. When starting your ecommerce business, avoid these people.

Anytime I start a new project, I share it with a few close friends and family members who are encouragers, not naysayers. I don't need to hear how someone else tried a similar strategy, and it didn't work out for them. Or it sounds like a scam. Or no one makes money in ecommerce anymore. Or why would you risk a steady income job for something like dropshipping?

As I wrote earlier, you will never know everything there is to know about dropshipping.

But I trust this book has given you the basic knowledge and confidence to get started. Trying anything for the first time can be scary and overwhelming. Everything worth doing usually is.

Take your success into your own hands and get started. Be bold and take action.

I love this quote by Kobi Yamada, a motivator of millions and New York Times bestselling author. I believe it applies to nearly any endeavor we try.

"Sometimes you just have to take the leap and build your wings on the way down."

This is a journey. Success won't come overnight, but if you stick with it, never give up, and focus on your end game, it will come.

Take your leap and relish every success along the way. Relish the failures as well. You learn more from those anyway.

The End

Before You Go

If you enjoyed this book and found it helpful in moving forward with your dropshipping journey, please consider leaving a review on Amazon. Reviews help make books readily available to other ecommerce entrepreneurs who may benefit from them.

Also, if you would like to see a book on another topic in the ecommerce or dropshipping niches, please send me an email at caitlyn@caitlynrich dot com and let me know. I'll do my best to provide the information readers want and need.

I always look forward to hearing from readers and coming up with new ways to enable them to achieve their dreams. Creating a passive income is the Number One goal for every one of us in ecommerce. I want to do as much as I can to make it possible for all those interested.

Added Bonus

Enjoy this Dropshipping Cheat Sheet that will help insure you've crossed all your T's and dotted your I's when building your drop-shipping empire and beginning to live the Ecommerce Lifestyle.

How would you like to get your store start-ed even faster and be even more successful? That's exactly what this cheat sheet is intended to help you with. These are secrets, tips and tricks that aren't included in the book that will help you to get to your goal faster and take some shortcuts that you ordinarily wouldn't have used. There are quite a few of them so let's get started.

1. Use your entire 15-day Shopify trial.

Often new store owners are so excited to get started that they will sign up for one of the plans that Shopify offers and will lose the days of their trial. The trial is intended to allow you to evaluate the platform completely without any cost or obligation.

2. Unless you are very familiar with

analytics systems and have a favorite already, stick with Google Analytics. It is one of the most useful analytics platforms on the web, and integrates with things like your Adwords account to help you advertise if you choose to do so.

3. Don't think, just do.

Many people want to consult experts in the field or the web for advice and get discouraged before they even start but the most successful entrepreneurs didn't think about it too much – they just believed they would be successful and they were.

4. Start as early as possible.

You might not be able to travel back in time and start yesterday, but you can start right now. You are going to need as much preparation time as possible and even if you aren't planning on launching your store for months you need to start right away.

5. One of the smartest things you can do

when it comes to products is to test a product before you purchase a single unit of it. Create a product listing or a group of listings and make them out of stock. Then, use whatever market-ing means you have, or whatever advertising campaigns that you can get on the cheap to get your products in front of a few people. Find out if there is truly some interest in the products that you are thinking about selling. You'll be able to look at your site analytics and see just how popular something is, and whether or not it is a worthwhile investment without having to buy a single unit. Since you are going to be buying in bulk to get wholesale prices, you need to be absolutely sure that you're going to be successful.

6. Ask for feedback

and don't ignore it. This seems like it is in di-rect contradiction with the advice in number three, but that's not the case. You aren't asking for advice here – you are asking for feedback on what you have already decided upon, and you're getting it from customers. In fact, no matter what it is that you are planning to sell, get advice on the product from customers as quickly as you can. The right advice could keep you from selling a product that is going to cost you money – or at least won't make you as much money as another product would – but customers will give you feedback right away if you ask for it.

7. Don't let your lack of experience

with ecommerce stop you from taking a great idea online. With Shopify, you have a much easier way of getting your product to consumers than if you were getting your ecommerce website online on your own. Even if you know nothing about ecommerce, with the *Shopify Secrets* book and all of the tips and information that is included here you'll be able to get your site online and running and you can turn that million dollar idea in to a million dollar business. From taking the payments to order fulfillment via third-party services, Shopify is the easiest platform to take your marketing ideas online.

8. Start small

until you know what products are going to be the most popular and which products are going to sell rarely if at all. For example, if you have a product that you are planning to offer in five different styles, ten different colors and four different sizes, you are looking at a total of 200 different products just to have one of each and the odds are that you probably won't sell most of the styles, sizes and colors for a long time. Start small, do your research and once you know what is selling big and what is never selling, then you can start placing your orders, with the confidence to know that you won't collapse from a cash-flow problem like so many other ecommerce businesses.

9. Use social media,

but if you are selling products, you especially want to use Pinterest. Pinterest is one of the most effective ways of getting your products in front of people and since Shopify makes it incredibly easy for you to set up a buy button right on your Pinterest posts, there is no setup or reason not to make use of this incredible tool. Pinterest allows you to post pictures of your products and get people's attention and many ecommerce websites say that Pinterest gives them more referrals than any other website around. Of course, you also need to make sure that other social media is being used as well because Facebook and Twitter, as well as a few others, are still great sources for sales.

10. Don't use the same, boring marketing

techniques some companies today are still using. In this world of viral videos and unique marketing ideas, you want to be as interesting as you can when it comes to marketing. Being boring isn't going to be effective anymore. That kind of advertising just doesn't work. Instead, try to think of some really creative ways that you can market your products. You can even ask your customers for ideas and see what they can come up with. You'd be surprised how much a loyal customer is willing to help a store they like.

Another Bonus

This checklist will help make sure you have everything you need to start your Shopify store. Since we covered so much material in this book, you may be having a hard time remembering it all. This checklist will ensure you are ready to open your store. Print it out and check each item off one at a time as you get it done. Then you'll be ready to open your Shopify store, and you'll be primed for success, wealth, and independence from your day job from the very beginning.

1. Payment Gateways

The first thing you'll want to check off your list is your payment gateway. Obviously, if you have no payment gateway, you have no ability to make sales. Not only do you need to make sure you have chosen all of the payment gateways you should have and configured them properly, you also need to make sure they're working properly by testing them individually a few times. Many stores have reached their launch date and spent advertising money only to discover they had a technical problem with their payment gateways and no one could buy anything. Don't test your payment gateways a few days before your launch. Do this several weeks before. It's totally frustrating to be ready to open for business only to realize you can't take your customers' money. Ugh!

2. The Shipping & Fulfillment System

If you're selling physical goods then you are going to need to have a shipping system in place. Luckily, Shopify makes this easier than most platforms. Still, it isn't something you want to leave to chance. Test out your shipping system several weeks in advance and make sure if you are using a dropshipper or a third-party to fulfill your orders they are sending products out on time. Your customers will remember little else about their shopping experience and the product they purchased from you other than shipping time. It's the number one thing that will influence someone's decision to buy from you again in the future. If you are doing your own order fulfilment make sure you have a plan for getting your orders out.

3. Search Engine Optimization

Since you are using Shopify you have a decided advantage when it comes to Search Engine Optimization. Still, this is one of the most important aspects of your store, since it represents your marketing efforts and determines where you'll fall in the search engine results. Also, this is where you want to set up your social media, and make sure you are following good practices like consistency and value building with your social media posts. Make sure each of your social media accounts is branded with your store—did I mention earlier the importance of branding?—so if a customer who knows you visits any one of them they will instantly recognize the look as your own.

4. Submit Your Sitemap

If you want your store to be entered in Google and other search engines correctly you are going to need to submit a sitemap. Shopify makes this process very easy. You can access your sitemap by going to name-of-your-site.myshopify.com/sitemap.xml. You might have thousands of product pages that need to be indexed in Google so submit your sitemap early and then do searches to make sure you can find everything. This will also give you some clues on whether or not you need to change your titles and HTML descriptions on some pages and whether you are optimized for the keywords you're intending to rank for.

5. Setting up Your Domain

You'll want to make sure your domain is set up properly. This is an important step, but sometimes people get confused and try to route the domain using third-party services when it fact you can easily set this up right through Shopify. Shopify will allow you to enter your name into the system and then whenever a web server makes a request for that domain, they will redirect them to your Shopify site. The process is fairly straightforward, and if you need help you can check out the HELP information on Shopify on domain forwarding.

6. Choosing the Right Tags

You'll need to use meta tags to teach the search engines what your pages are about. The meta tags tell the search engines what the title of a page is, as well as give it a description. When you type in a keyword phrase in Google, notice it is highlighted in the page description on all of the search results that contain it. Obviously, that means you also need to include the keyword the page is about in your description. Although Shopify does have some powerful tools for doing search engine optimization on your site there are actually better third-party applications that can ensure your site pages are tagged correctly.

7. Make Sure Your Site Works on Mobile Devices

This is probably the most important item to get off of your checklist in this modern age – other than your payment options. The mobile device is the way modern consumers are buying. If you don't have a responsive theme displaying your site correctly on all the major mobile devices on the market, your sales are going to suffer. You can test whether or not your site works on mobile devices from tablets to iPhones by looking up mobile testing sites. These are very accurate and can help you see what your page looks like on a specific device.

In addition, you need to make sure your payments are working on mobile devices. This is a mistake often made by new storeowners. They check their payment settings and gateways for functionality through the computer, but they don't test out payments made on a mobile device. Remember, you need to test out your gateway on mobile for each of the payment gateways you set up. Part of this is display, but most of it is whether or not the payment will actually work on a mobile device. This is something you should work out several weeks before you launch your site.

Other Books
by

Caitlyn Rich

the Ecommerce Lifestyle Series

Dropshipping: The Ultimate Guide to Building an Ecommerce Business & Earning Passive Income Online

Blow Up Your Shopify Store & Turn it Into a Money Making Machine

Dropshipping: How to Brand your Ecommerce Business & Make More Money

Than Ever Before

Coming Soon

Dropshipping and the Millionaire Mindset: How to Achieve Financial Freedom in Ecommerce by Changing Your Habits.

In this exciting fourth installment of the *Ecommerce Lifestyle Series*, I'll show you how you can develop a Millionaire Mindset by changing your attitude and habits and earn massive revenue with your Ecommerce business.

"You do not decide your future. You decide your habits and your habits decide your future." – Dan Lock

Why do some of us become millionaires while the majority of the world stays broke? Why does it seem like some people can turn anything they touch into gold while the same idea turns to garbage in another person's hands? How can dropshipping make millionaires out of some while 90% of the rest go out of business in a week?

Is it the system that failed? Is it Dropshipping or Amazon FBA or Affiliate Marketing or whatever other flavor of the month we're chasing?

What do all the ecommerce winners have in common and what can we learn from them?

In *Dropshipping and the Millionaire Mindset*, I'll expose the methods and techniques highly successful people utilize to build wealth, create passive income, and achieve financial freedom. I'll show you how to apply millionaire mindset principals and techniques to your business so you can recognize the success saboteurs that rob you of your ability to build wealth and end their reign in your life and business forever.

By developing a millionaire mindset, you can become like all the successful dropshippers and ecommerce giants who changed their lives and the world around them. You, too, can achieve financial independence, build wealth, and start living life your way.

Right now.

About Caitlyn

Caitlyn Rich is an online entrepreneur, author, and teacher. She lives in Ohio where she is active in animal rescue, her local church, running, travel, and taking care of a large property that has become her oasis in a crazy world. As always, she is busy writing more books to equip and encourage aspiring entrepreneurs to achieve their own goals, as well as find joy and contentment, regardless of where they are in their ecommerce journey.

Follow Caitlyn on Facebook or her website, *Ecommerce Lifestyle*, and sign up for updates on new titles and trainings.